OPEN WIDE AND SAY... HA!

A Selection of Humorous Stories from a Pediatrician's Office

LYNDA GREENBERG

Copyright © 2013 Lynda Greenberg

All rights reserved.

ISBN: 1490527745

ISBN 13: 9781490527741

Library of Congress Control Number: 2013912175
CreateSpace Independent Publishing Platform
North Charleston, South Carolina

AUTHOR BIOGRAPHY

Lynda Greenberg taught preschool for twenty years in Calgary, Alberta; Vancouver, British Columbia; and Toronto, Ontario, before deciding on a career change. Although Lynda loved teaching, she was intrigued at the thought of working with her husband as well as trying something new. That's when Lynda made the change from teaching to become a medical secretary and office manager. She began working in her husband's pediatric practice fourteen years ago and has never looked back!

Lynda lives happily in Thornhill, Ontario, Canada, with her husband of thirty-six years. Dr. Manny and Lynda have three children and eleven grandchildren, whom they adore.

This collection of stories from our office has been accumulating on notepads and little scraps of paper for many years.

Judy Bando, who was one of our original office nurses, was the first one to come up with the idea of writing down amusing stories as they happened. As years went by, other staff members continued adding their tales to the notepads, which grew by the week. Some days I felt I needed to have my own secretary just to keep up with the stories that needed to be recorded! Many thanks to all my coworkers, past and present, who contributed.

A huge thanks goes to Barb, my partner in crime at the front desk; Jaycee, our very capable secretarial assistant; and to our wonderful nurses, Andi, Gabi, and Carmina. Together, no matter how busy the office gets, we manage to find time to laugh and to keep a sense of humor through it all; it's what keeps us sane. Last but not least, many thanks to a very good friend with whom I recently reconnected from my college days, Peggy Zabol Schwarzmer, for coming up with the title for this book.

I would also like to give a "shout out" to my illustrator, Jordan Ockrant. Jordan has attended three years of animation in a private Toronto college specializing in representational art and animation. He has worked on advertising animation, billboard illustrations, character design, and illustration for special occasions and portraits. Jordan is a real pleasure to work with and somehow magically was able to transform the pictures I had in my mind onto paper! Jordan can be contacted by e-mail at jordan_ockrant@hotmail.com.

Of course none of the real names of the families and children have been used in any of these tales. Where a name is used, it is fictitious, unless it's my name or my husband's, whom I commonly refer to in the stories as "Dr. Manny."

I don't even know where to begin to thank Manny, who is not only my husband but also my very best friend. Together we have shared thousands of hours of laughter over the years, both at the office and at home. Laughter is a huge part of our lives, and I can't think of a day that has gone by in our thirty-six years of marriage that we haven't shared something funny with each other.

*This book is dedicated to our pediatric patients,
big and small, as well as their moms, dads, and
grandparents, who give us a reason to look forward to
going to work every day!*

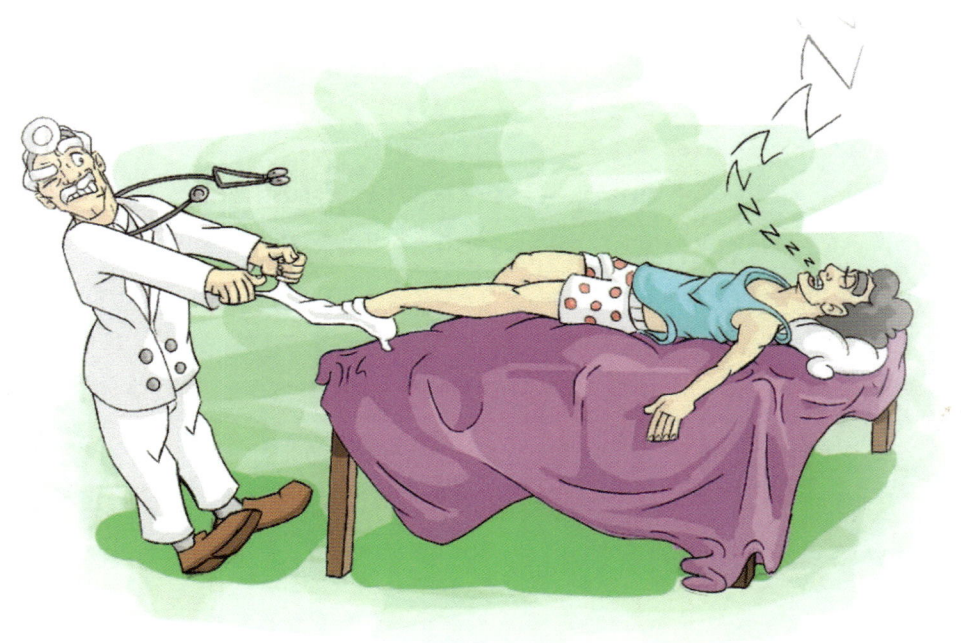

QUESTIONS FOR THE STAFF/APPOINTMENT REQUESTS

On a busy day at the office, we usually receive close to two hundred phone calls. These calls are usually general requests for simple appointments and test results. However there are exceptions to this rule, as you will see in the stories below.

A mom called the office in desperation to ask if I could please get her teenager's doctor on the phone right away. She said that her teen refused to get out of bed, and perhaps speaking with the doctor would help. I told her the doctor couldn't get his own teenagers out of bed, much less anyone else's kid.

***

A mother called to book an appointment with the doctor for her two-month-old, who "gets headaches when it rains," which causes him to cry.

***

A very anxious mother called the office about her two-year-old daughter having a glow-in-the-dark-colored urine. It was bright yellow, and she was getting more worried by the second as she checked the Internet as to what ghastly diseases could cause this. We got her into the office within an hour and gave her a urine cup to get a test sample. The urine did have a rather scary-looking color to it. However when it was tested, there was nothing alarming to see. Dr. Manny took off the diaper and examined the area. It turned out the little one had gotten her hands on a yellow highlighter marker and had colored herself in a very interesting area of her body. All the urine passing through there had turned bright fluorescent yellow. Dr. Manny took an alcohol swab and wiped the area clean. Poor mom was rather mortified. This mom happened to be our daughter, and the patient was our granddaughter.... which goes to show these things can happen to anyone, even a pediatrician's daughter!

***

Mom wanted to bring her eighteen-month-old in for fever caused by stress.

***

"I'd like to book an appointment. Chelsea hasn't been breathing for over a week now."

***

"My two-year-old had her ears pierced ten months ago and now needs an MRI and needs to remove them. Will her ear piercing holes close up?"

***

A two-year-old had a bleeding diaper rash and refused to let mom change her diaper. Therefore she is in the same wet diaper all day. What should Mother do?

***

"Am I allowed to bring my child to the office in pajamas?"

***

A mom called the office to say she wanted to check us out before committing to us as patients. Specifically, she needed to see if we had "good toys."

***

A child splashed clean water on himself from the toilet bowl. Should he come in and be examined by the doctor?

***

A dad would like a blood test for his child for SARS because he ate Chinese food last month.

***

A parent phoned to ask if it was all right to dip her three-month-old son's pacifier in wine to help the baby sleep.

***

A mom called to cancel an appointment for a fever because the fever was gone. She wanted to speak to the nurse to ask why the fever was gone because she wanted an explanation from her as to what had been wrong.

***

Mother said she wanted to know if she should keep her sick visit that was booked for her baby. She asked the nurse if she thought he would be sick all day, or would he feel better later?

***

A mother asked for a "written guarantee" that the doctor would not keep her waiting more than ten minutes because she had to get to work.

***

We received a concerned phone call from a father who said when he pulled his eight-year-old son's sweatshirt over his head while helping him get dressed, he had jerked it hard. Did the doctor think his son could get brain damage? Perhaps an MRI would be a good idea? When asked if his son was in pain, the dad said, "I don't think so. He's at school."

***

Mother called because her nine-month-old needs an appointment because she is having hallucinations.

***

Mom needed to book an appointment because she feared her poor twelve-month-old baby had yet another ear infection. She said, "She hasn't been herself since the day she was born."

***

Dad called to make an appointment about his six-month-old baby's "bad behavior" and declared that his son was very "manipulative."

***

Mom asked nurse if she could "catch something" if she took a bite of her daughter's sandwich after the child received a measles shot.

***

Mom wanted to bring in her child who has a fever. She says he got it from drinking very cold water.

***

Dad said his two-year-old daughter was hoarse. He wanted to know if that could happen from swallowing a chicken bone. When asked when the child had swallowed a chicken bone, dad said she didn't. He was just wondering.

***

Mom called upset that her child had been ill for a week with a very sore throat and fever. She was unhappy with her doctor, who hadn't managed to make her child feel better. She said she wanted to see one of the other doctors in our office to get a second opinion. When I explained that we don't move patients from one doctor to another within our office unless their own pediatrician is away, she said, "OK, I guess I'll try the doctor's recommendations to take the antibiotics then. Maybe that will help."

***

A woman called to say her nephew was coming in for a checkup. She asked us to do a DNA test. She didn't believe her brother was the father.

***

A thirteen-year-old boy called to see if he could shadow the doctor for a school project. I asked his name, and whether he was a patient in the office, as I didn't see his name in our files. He said he's not, but his mom told him to tell the secretary that their family is very good friends with the doctor's family, so it should be fine. When I said I was married to the doctor and had no idea who his family was, he said, "OK. Thanks anyway. My mom said you might say that."

***

A father called requesting an appointment for his son because of a possible infection in his "private parts." He was told that his regular doctor was away and was given the option of seeing another doctor instead. Dad said he only wanted his son to see a male physician because it's embarrassing for him to see a female doctor for this personal issue. How old was this patient? Six weeks.

***

Mom: My teenager saw the doctor two months ago for a concussion. Since then he's been failing math and science. Can I get a letter for his teacher saying the doctor recommends he cut back on his workload?

Me: How was he doing in math and science before the concussion?

Mom: Not so good.

***

I booked an appointment, and after I hung up, I couldn't remember the reason for the appointment, which we must put into the schedule so the doctors know what to expect. Therefore, in the space reserved for the reason, I put "can't remember," assuming that Barb, the other secretary, would ask them when they came in and document it at that time. When the mom brought the child in for the appointment, Barb asked if her child had amnesia. "No, she has a stomach ache," said the mom. "Why on earth would you think she has amnesia?" "Because," said the secretary, "Lynda put that the reason you booked this appointment was because your daughter can't remember."

***

Twenty minutes before their appointment, a father called to cancel his two-month-old daughter's checkup because "she's refusing to go into the car seat."

***

Dad called to book an appointment because his three-year-old fell on his head and had a large bump. He said he was on his way to the office, but was there something he should do in the meantime? I told him the doctor said to take a bag of frozen peas, and hold it against the bump. Dad called back five minutes later to say he couldn't find frozen peas; will mixed frozen vegetables be OK?

***

Dad called, saying he received a call from his six-year-old daughter's camp. She was found eating mushrooms that were growing outside. After I gave the father the phone number to Poison Control, he said, "I can't get her to eat a single vegetable at home. But at camp she's picking them out of the grass and eating them!"

***

WHY DO PATIENTS THINK I HAVE ALL THE ANSWERS?

I often think that some of the calls we get in the office have hidden cameras involved, and I am being victimized for some sort of reality show. It is always interesting to me that some parents seem to think that we have all the information at our fingertips as to their children's program hours, whether it's ballet class, swimming lessons, or anything else. With more than five thousand patients in our office, that would be a very cool trick!

Here are some examples of the questions I have heard over the years, many of which I had no answers for!

"I left my diaper bag in my locked car in the parking lot. What are the chances it will get stolen?"

***

Mom called to book a summer physical for her daughter. She asked me what time I thought her child would be finished at camp.

***

A patient's mom called that she had an appointment with the ENT (ear, nose, and throat) specialist that afternoon. This particular specialist had cancelled their last two appointments, the mother told me. Did I think she should go or just assume he would cancel this one also?

***

A mom called at 9:20 a.m. "I have a three fifty appointment today. Do you think it's going to be raining then?"

***

"I have an appointment next Wednesday at four. Do you think there will be a parking spot open?"

***

Mom was making an appointment for Monday at 9:30 a.m. What did I think the traffic would be like on the main streets at that time? And how long would it take her to drive to the office from her house?

***

Mom called from the parking lot and said, "I've been on hold for fifteen minutes, and I had an appointment ten minutes ago! I need to ask you something before I come up. Do you think it's OK to leave my tomatoes in the car in this weather?"

***

Mom needed an appointment with the doctor for her child on Friday, but she had her own dentist appointment. How long did I think she'll be at the dentist?

***

A mother called to get results of a blood test. I explained that the results had come in and that once the doctor let me know what they were, I would call her back. She asked why I couldn't just read the results to her. I responded, "I wouldn't be able to tell you that; they're Greek to me!" She then asked, "The results come back in Greek?"

***

A parent booked an appointment for a month from now and asked if the doctor would be running on time.

***

Mom called on a busy Friday to ask for a phone number of a twenty-four-hour dry cleaner. She was going away on Sunday and needed a dress dry cleaned for her trip.

***

A patient's mother stopped me at a convenience store on a weekend to ask me which specialist her child was referred to and when was the appointment. I explained that I don't actually carry the appointment schedule with me everywhere I go.

***

A mom called to book an appointment on a Thursday for her sick child. When I offered her 3:20 p.m., she replied, "Don't you remember I have car pool on Thursdays at that time?"

***

ABOVE AND BEYOND THE CALL OF DUTY?

I am often asked questions that leave me completely speechless, despite the fact that I am not well known for being short on words! I suppose most parents don't realize how busy we are at the office; we book approximately 150 patients a day, answer about 200 calls a day, and respond to about 80 e-mails a day. Here are some examples of the many head-scratching questions we have heard!

When booking a flu shot for a child, I asked the mom if the child had egg allergies (because there is egg white in the flu shot). Mom asked, "Why do you ask? Are you going to be serving breakfast at the flu shot clinic?"

***

Although the office is very busy and we rarely get a minute to take a break, we have been asked occasionally to call a taxi to take a patient home after their appointment is over. Despite being so overwhelmed, we understand that not every patient has a cell phone to call their own taxi, so we are happy to help out. But this was a first: a mother called me from home to say she's ready to leave her house for the office for her baby's checkup. Can I please call a taxi to pick them up and bring them to the office? I asked the mom if she was already taking the time to phone ME to call a taxi to pick her up, why didn't she simply call the taxi directly herself? Mom sheepishly replied that she had never thought of that, thanked me, and said she would make the call.

***

Then there are the parents who really don't want to bother coming to the office at all, whether by taxi or car. A mom called and said she would like the doctor to come to her house to do the four-month checkup so the baby wasn't exposed to sick patients in the office. She had a scale, she explained, so the doctor could just bring his stethoscope and anything else he felt necessary.

***

A mother called that she would like the name and phone number of the parent who was sitting next to her in the office waiting room yesterday. She said she could give me the friend's child's name and the time he was seen, to narrow it down for me. When I said that this is confidential information, and I was not at liberty to share patient information, she said she was an old high school friend whose last name she doesn't know. She understood why I couldn't give her the details. So, she asked, could I then please call the woman and give her *her* contact information? In my spare time, of course.

***

Another doctor's secretary shared this story with me: She received a call from a patient saying she needed to pick up her glasses from the optometrist next door to the doctor's. However the optometrist closes at 5:00 p.m., and the patient would still be at work. She said she knows that their medical office also closes at 5:00 p.m., but would she mind picking them up for her from next door and staying later until she gets there to pick them up? She shouldn't be later than 5:45 p.m.

***

WRONG NUMBERS AND PHONE CALLS GONE AWRY

Sometimes it can be very difficult to hear what is being said on the phone. The combination of background office noise together with a host of other reasons can create confusion that makes for some interesting conversations.

Me (to new patient on the phone): What is your child's first name?

Mom: Wance.

Me: Wance? How do you spell that?

Mom: Wee, a, n, c, e

Me: What is that first letter again?

Mom: Wee.

Me: Sorry, but there is no such letter as "wee" in the alphabet.

Mom: Yes there is. Wee, a, n, c, e.

Me: I'm sorry. I don't understand. Can you give me a word beginning with that letter?

Mom: Yes. Wance.

Me: How about a different word?

Mom: Wee. For Wictor.

***

Mom (in heavy accent): I need appointment for my son. He has information in his belly button.

Me: Do you mean an inflammation?

Mom: No, I mean "information."

***

A secretary in another pediatrician's office told me this story:

Parent: I've been on hold for ten minutes. Finally you answer!

Secretary: Sorry, but it's very busy here. What can I do for you?

Parent: I wanted to know what the weather was like today.

Secretary: Why would you call a doctor's office to ask that?

Parent: Well *you've* been out. I haven't!

***

Caller: Is this Dr. Goldbloom's office?

Me: No, you have the wrong number. We have four doctors working here but nobody by that name.

Caller: Can you please give me Dr. Goldbloom's phone number then?

Me: I don't know who he is.

Caller: He's a doctor in your building. Of course you must have his number! He's in your building!

I thought for a while and then asked the caller:

Me: Can you please give me Mr. Brown's phone number?

Caller: Who is Mr. Brown?

Me: Your neighbor. You must have his number. He lives right next door to you!

[click]

***

A three-week-old baby came into the office and was having difficulty breathing. The doctor asked me to call 911 immediately to get an ambulance to take the baby to the hospital. This is how the conversation went:

911: Nine-one-one, how may I direct your call?

Me: Ambulance please.

911: What is the nature of your call?

Me: I am calling from a pediatrician's office about a three-week-old baby with labored breathing.

911: OK, ma'am, an ambulance is on the way. Meanwhile I need to ask you some questions.

First, does the patient seem confused?

Me: Confused? He's three weeks old. I don't know what a confused three-week-old baby looks like. For that matter, I don't know what a non-confused three-week-old baby looks like.

911: Ma'am. These are questions I must ask you as part of our protocol.

Me: OK. Go ahead.

911: Is the patient having chest pain?

Me: Well, I wouldn't know. As he's only three weeks old, he's not speaking much yet.

911: Ma'am. This is protocol. Please answer the question.

Me: The answer would be "I don't know."

911: Is the patient dizzy or lightheaded?

Me: You are asking me questions as if I'm calling about an adult having a heart attack or stroke. Do you not have a different list to read questions from for children and babies?

911: No, ma'am. We only have one list. Never mind. The ambulance is outside your door. Thank you.

***

Our office had a service where parents could call and speak to a doctor on the phone about their children if they were ill outside of regular office hours. On our answering machine, parents were instructed to call another number, which then forwarded the call to the physician's pager who was on call that evening.

Unfortunately, the forwarding phone number we stated on our recorded message was often misunderstood by the parents. In fact, the same lady called us numerous times and asked us to please pronounce our forwarding number more clearly, as she was receiving calls from distraught parents to her home phone number on a regular basis in the evenings. Her phone number was only one number off from our forwarded phone number. We really did try to remedy this problem; however, we often were making recorded messages with crying children in the background, and once again we were receiving calls from Mrs. J. begging us to please speak more clearly. Eventually I got a call from a very fed-up and exasperated Mrs. J. "I give up!" she said. "Last night I got yet another call from an upset mother. She was going on and on about her baby having a fever, and then a rash breaking out on his skin. I could not get a word in edgewise. This mother was not the least bit interested in hearing me tell her she had the wrong number, and that I was not the pediatrician on call. Anyway, I told her it sounds like her baby had roseola and suggested she contact her pediatrician in the morning."

***

On Sunday mornings, we run an emergency clinic for all the patients in the office. The answering machine message states, "This Sunday, Dr. Manny is holding an emergency clinic for sick children only. If your child is ill, please call back on Sunday morning or e-mail for an appointment." One Sunday morning I answered the phone and the woman on the other end shouted, "What number am I? Is it too late to get my child seen? What number am I?" I asked her what she was talking about. She said the answering machine said we are holding an emergency clinic for *six* children only. She was worried that she wouldn't get in before all six appointments were taken.

MEDICATIONS AND PRESCRIPTIONS

I am not sure why there seem to be so many questions about medications after the doctors have already made their diagnoses. Perhaps parents are worried about their children who are ill and therefore not really paying close attention to the doctor's directions.

A mother called the office to tell me that a doctor from a house-call service came to their house last night to check on their ill child. He phoned in a prescription for antibiotics for her child. Which pharmacy do I think this doctor would have called it in to? She can't remember.

***

Mom: "The prescription instructions say 'keep out of sunlight.' Does that mean my child, or the medication?"

Me: "'Keep out of Sunlight' refers to the medication. The bottle also says 'Shake Vigorously,' and 'Keep Refrigerated.' That also refers to the medication."

***

"We paid for the varivax [chickenpox] vaccine, and a few months later my child got the chickenpox. Is there a money-back guarantee I can get from the pharmacy?"

***

Medications and Prescriptions

A mother saw an advertisement on television for some kind of medication for babies that said, "Ask your doctor to prescribe it." She doesn't remember what it was. Maybe the doctor knows?

***

A four-month-old baby spit out the vitamins he was given. His mom asked if she could give him chewables.

***

The doctor gave a parent two prescriptions for her baby. One was for a cream to be used on the skin for a yeast infection. The other was for a meningitis shot from the pharmacy that the nurse was to administer at the next appointment. Mom called me a few days later and said, "I picked up the prescriptions at the pharmacy, but I am a bit confused. I had a very difficult time opening that cork that came in the vial. I finally got it open, and I poured it over my daughter's skin. Now I have this cream left. I don't know what I'm supposed to do with that."

***

A mother came out of the room after seeing the doctor and said she forgot to ask him to write a note for the daycare saying he allowed them to give the child medication when needed. I explained to the mom that the doctor wouldn't write notes like that, and that the parent was the one who must give permission to the daycare to use over-the-counter medication. She then said she would need a note from the doctor stating that he's not giving them a note. When I told her there would be a charge for a note saying he's not giving a note, she declned.

***

IN THE EXAMINING ROOM

This is where many of our interesting stories start out. Of course, I am not in the examining room with the patients, so the doctors and nurses have passed these tales on to me.

Mom came for an emergency sick visit appointment with a perfectly healthy five-year-old child. However a stranger in the mall told her that her son looked ill, so she thought she better bring him to the office to be checked by the doctor.

***

Mom held on tightly to her four-month-old son on the examining table because "he has a fear of heights."

***

The doctor tried to listen to a screaming child with his stethoscope. The child's mom tried to talk to the doctor at the same time. He said he was trying to listen to the child's chest and couldn't hear, which was a nice way of asking mom not to talk to him at that moment. So the mom started shouting at the top of her lungs.

***

A mom wanted the nurse to do the six-month shot without taking off the baby's winter coat. "He'll get upset."

***

The doctor prescribed medication for pinworm for a four-year-old child. The mother looked at the prescription and asked if her child would get liver disease. Dr. Manny said as long as he doesn't use drugs or drink alcohol, then he'd probably be OK.

***

A particularly long-winded parent had been in the examining room with my husband for almost an hour. I knocked on the door and apologized for interrupting. I said we only had one car here, and I really needed to get home. The dad said, "No problem. You take the doc's car, and we'll give him a ride home when we're done here."

***

A mother abruptly left in the middle of a physical examination of her four-month-old son to take the baby to the washroom. She said she was toilet training him, and the first step was to take him into a bathroom when she thinks he's about to make a bowel movement and hold him over the toilet.

***

A newborn baby was booked for a checkup. When the nurse called the name for the baby to be brought into the room to be weighed and measured, the mother said she didn't bring the baby with her. When asked why not, she replied, "I'm not bringing a newborn out in this weather!" She said she could tell us anything we might want to know about her baby, and she didn't need to have the child present for a checkup.

***

Parents of a newborn baby arrived at the office for a routine first-month checkup. The father asked the doctor how to start teaching the baby to read. The doctor explained that the baby is only one month of age, so why did he think it was time to teach him to read? Mom interjected, "So why is there a poster in the waiting room that says, 'Literacy Begins at Birth'?"

***

A very pregnant mother came in for yearly checkups for her six-year-old twin daughters. After the examinations were complete, the mother turned to the doctor and asked him if he would mind doing "a quick internal examination" on her to see if she was in labor.

***

After seeing the doctor with her child who had a rash, the mom came out of the examining room and, in front of Dr. Manny, said to me, "Lynda, the doctor says he has roseola. But I'd like to know what *you* think."

***

My hubby was taking an extraordinary amount of time with a patient I had booked for a relatively simple problem. I got some nasty looks from parents in the waiting room who were making sure I noticed them checking their watches every minute. Finally I sent an instant message through the computer system to him asking if he would be much longer because the parents in the waiting room were getting impatient. When he came out, he stopped in front of my desk and said quietly, "Lynda, you must know that when I spend more time than usual with a patient, there's a reason. I'm not just doing it for the fun of it. Some things simply need more time." Then the mom came out of the room and proudly proclaimed to me and the entire waiting room, "I just taught your husband how to make sushi!"

***

Mom wanted to book her five-month-old baby's next checkup after just completing the four-month checkup. I noticed that Manny had not been in the best mood because we had just encountered a major problem with our computer system. He was frustrated that this computer issue had taken valuable time out of his day. As a result, he was running behind and frantically trying to catch up. I was hoping the parents of the patients hadn't noticed that he wasn't his usual happy self. When I asked what time mother would like for the next appointment, she said, "Preferably in the morning. He's kind of cranky in the afternoon." I apologized on my husband's behalf and told her the doctor had a rough afternoon with computer issues, and perhaps that's why he was cranky.

Mom replied, "I wasn't talking about the doctor being cranky in the afternoon. I was referring to my baby."

***

A mother brought her very overweight nine-year-old daughter to see the doctor because she was, she claimed, "at her wit's end" trying to figure out why she was gaining weight so rapidly. According to the mom, the child ate only healthy foods: fruits, vegetables, whole wheat breads. The pounds were rapidly piling on, and she was at a loss as to what to do. The doctor gave mom a two-week eating plan for her daughter to follow, and asked her to come back to reassess the situation. The young girl had brought her lunch box to the appointment because she was on her way to school. As she jumped down from the examining table with it, she dropped it, and it opened up, spilling out the contents. The lunch box contained three large chocolate bars and a bag with half a dozen cookies. The mother's face turned bright red. She looked at the doctor and said, "Well, we do like to give her little treats once in a while!"

AND THEN THERE ARE THE DADS...

Often when the fathers come to the office with their children, they look like they'd rather be having a root canal than bringing their kids to the pediatrician's office. Their eyes dart around the waiting room, and they look like deer caught in headlights. Often these dads are clutching raggedy notes with lists of questions from mom for the doctor to answer. Manny says in all his years of practicing medicine, he has never had a mother arrive with a note or instructions from the father!

Most of the time, these dads practically run out of the office when the appointment is finished, obviously relieved to have it over with. Until, of course, they get home to mom. Invariably, mom calls the office an hour later with irritation in her voice. She wants to know what happened at the appointment, and dad doesn't seem to remember.

Dad brought in passport applications for his five-year-old and seven-year-old for the doctor to sign. He asked me to help him finish the forms and to answer questions he didn't know the answers to before getting the doctor's signature. For example: What color are their eyes? I was quite surprised by this question and asked him when he last saw his children. Dad said this morning at breakfast. He just didn't notice.

**

A father brought a child in for a pre-op, an examination the surgeon requests the pediatrician to do before surgery is performed. This is to ensure the child is healthy for the upcoming operation. The doctor asked what kind of operation his child was having. Dad had no clue.

***

Dad called to cancel his two-year-old child's checkup that afternoon. The reason? "The child refuses to come."

***

Dad: "Is it OK to feed a child who is teething?"

***

Dad called to see if the doctor would sign as the guarantor for the passport of his one-year-old child. I asked him if they had any other children because the doctor must know the family, if not this particular child, for at least two years in order to sign the passport. Dad said he didn't know. He had to ask his wife.

***

The Jewish doctor was going to be doing a routine circumcision on a Catholic child. The mother called back three times to make sure that a Jewish doctor performing a circumcision couldn't cause their child to become Jewish.

***

WALK-INS AND "EMERGENCIES"

Although we have three telephone lines and an e-mail service used for booking appointments, there are still parents who walk in with their children without appointments. As we pride ourselves on booking appropriately and running pretty much on time, we frown on walk-ins and usually have to tell them to come back at a later time because there are other people waiting who have booked time with their doctors. Alternatively they can wait and see if someone else comes late, and we'll add them in.

Mom told us she called 911 because her child was in pain from teething. She couldn't understand why the ambulance refused to take her to the hospital, so she walked into our office without an appointment and said she needed to be seen right then.

***

A mother arrived with her child without booking an appointment. When told she needed to book one because we were not a walk-in clinic, she asked how much she could pay me in order to be seen right away.

***

A mother walked in with her five-year-old daughter without an appointment and demanded to see the doctor. When told that the doctor was busy with booked patients, and she could have an appointment in an hour or so, she said that wasn't acceptable. She walked down the hall and started to open the door handle of the examining room that the doctor and patient were in! I told her under no circumstances could she walk into an examining room like that. She stood outside the door with her arms folded and said she would wait for the doctor right there. When Manny came out, I told him what had happened. "Mrs. Smith," he said. "All patients in this office must book appointments in order to be seen. We are not a walk-in clinic." Mrs. Smith replied, "So, are you telling me that you **never** will see a patient who does not have an appointment pre-booked? Ever!?" The doctor looked at her healthy-looking child and said, "I wouldn't say never. If a child came in with breathing difficulty or in the midst of a seizure, I certainly would see them right away." The mother responded, "Jessica! Have a seizure!"

***

MISUNDERSTANDINGS AND CONFUSION

A surgeon had written instructions for his patients before operations that included "Do not eat at home before surgery." The parent decided to stop at a restaurant for breakfast on the way to his child's surgery and fed him donuts and chocolate milk. They then proceeded to the hospital for the child's operation, where it was explained that the child actually couldn't eat breakfast *anywhere*. Not just at home.

***

I received a call from a very upset mother who said she was changing her three-month-old daughter's diaper and needed an immediate emergency appointment. She was in a complete panic and would only tell me that something "terrible" had happened to her baby's "private parts"—so terrible that she couldn't even explain it to me on the phone. I rushed her in for an appointment. The mother arrived shaking and crying. I took her into an examining room and tried to calm her down while she waited for the doctor to come in. The baby was happy, gurgling, and certainly did not seem to be in any type of distress. As Dr. Manny entered the room, the mother said, "Thank goodness you're here, Doctor! I don't know what to do! I'm so upset!" At that point I left the room and returned to my desk. After the appointment I asked Manny what on earth had happened that caused the mother to be so distraught. He told me that mom said she was cleaning the baby after she had a dirty diaper, and mom noticed the baby's "private area" had a hole in it. She tearfully asked him if the hole would eventually close up on its own. Dr. Manny replied that he certainly hoped not.

***

A newborn African American baby came with his mom for his first checkup. When asked for the baby's name, the mom said his name was Malebla (spelling it out). The pediatrician remarked, "That's a very unusual name. I've never heard it before. How do you pronounce it?" The mom replied, "We think it's Mal-EH-blah. But we don't really know. That's the name the hospital gave him." When the doctor asked what she meant by that, she said that when her son was brought to her in her hospital room for the first time after he was born, he was wearing a wristband that said MALEBLA on it. The mom went on to explain it wasn't their choice of names. They actually didn't really like it. The doctor explained that this stood for "Male Black," and that the parents were free to choose any name they liked. They left the office very happy, knowing that they didn't have to call their son Malebla for the rest of his life.

***

Although many of the families are aware that I am married to Manny, there are parents who are not. A mother of one of Manny's patient's told me she was at a party where there was a group standing around chatting about their pediatricians. When "Mrs. B" said her children's doctor is Dr. Manny, another mom responded with, "There's something off about that doctor. I've seen him acting very flirty with Lynda, the secretary. He calls her 'honey' and touches her shoulder. It's quite uncomfortable to see a doctor treating his secretary that way." Of course, Mrs. B explained to the mother that Dr. Manny is actually married to the secretary and has been for many years.

***

Aside from the four pediatricians working in our office, we also have an allergist who comes in every two weeks to see patients. A parent requested an appointment because her child was breaking out in hives after eating walnuts. The doctor asked me to instruct the parents to bring walnut butter to the appointment. The allergist said she would then rub some of the walnut butter directly on the skin to do the testing. Every week before the allergy appointments, my secretarial assistant, Jaycee, sends out e-mails to all of the patients coming in the following week. The e-mail informs them of their appointment time and which medicines they should avoid before the appointment that may affect the outcome of the testing. I asked Jaycee to please add to this particular patient's e-mail that they should not forget to bring walnut butter, or, if they couldn't find that, to bring in plain walnuts. To save time, Jaycee always cuts and pastes instructions for the allergy appointments into each e-mail, changing only the time slot, before sending them. A few weeks later, the first appointment of the day arrived to see the allergist. The mother handed me a jar of walnut butter. When she saw my perplexed face, she said her e-mail reminder told her to bring it, although she didn't really understand why it was necessary, as her daughter's allergies were to grass and pollen. I realized that Jaycee had mistakenly cut and pasted that one particular e-mail meant for the patient allergic to walnuts and sent it to everyone coming the following week. As the day progressed, the patients continued coming in with all types of walnuts: walnut butter, whole walnuts, walnuts in the shell, walnuts in urine cups. I guess it's true that Canadians are known for their politeness and willingness to listen to what they are told to do! We all decided that maybe for the next week's appointments, we would add into the e-mail not to forget to bring some nice cheese and a bottle of wine.

EXCUSES FOR MISSED APPOINTMENTS AND BEING LATE:

While the majority of parents arrive on time for their appointments, there are always those few who regularly come late or don't show up for their scheduled visits. We now have an e-mail service that sends out reminders the day before the appointment, so luckily we don't have as many no-shows as we used to. Unfortunately, though, we still have some who continue to miss many of their booked visits.

On the flip side, I'm fascinated by the parents who take the time to call and say they won't be coming when I would never expect them to! For example, a mother called from her labor room in between contractions to say she was unable to bring her four-year-old in for her checkup because she was having a baby any minute.

Here are some of the excuses parents have given for being late or missing their appointments completely. True or not, I don't know, but certainly original.

"I am locked in my garage because there's a power failure, and the garage door won't open."

***

"I am trying to leave for your office, but there is a huge unleashed dog sitting outside my house with no owner around. I am terrified to leave the house."

Excuses for Missed Appointments and Being Late

***

When I called a mother to tell her she missed her child's appointment, she explained, "I didn't come to the appointment with my child today because I have food poisoning. I didn't want anybody else in the waiting room to catch it from me."

***

A mother called that she was on her way to the office but would be about twenty minutes late. She got lost and realized she needed to turn around. Mom saw a funeral home on the corner, and decided she would drive into the lot and turn around through the other end of their driveway. Once she exited, she began driving down the street toward our office. Suddenly, she noticed a long line of cars behind her, all driving with their lights on. As she turned right at the next street light, the caravan of cars followed her. She made another quick turn, and again, the cars followed her. Mom realized that they thought she was leading the procession from the funeral home to the cemetery. She stopped her car, got out, and tapped on the window of the car behind her. "Excuse me," she said. "Are you following me?" The driver replied that he was. When she explained that she actually was not part of the funeral party, and was not driving to the cemetery but was just using the driveway to turn around, the driver became visibly upset. Now he was the front driver, and everyone was following him, thinking he was leading them to the cemetery. He had no idea where he was and felt responsible for the fifty or so cars waiting patiently behind him. She told me she would be running late because she felt obligated to help him navigate his way to the cemetery.

***

I had to contact a family who regularly missed their children's appointments without letting us know, to say they had missed another one. I explained to the father that unfortunately, we did have to bill for this missed physical because it was the third one in a row. In a quiet voice, the father said, "I do apologize. My mother-in-law died this morning. The last thing I was thinking of was bringing Julia to the doctor." I said I was so sorry to hear this sad news, and of course, we would not be billing them. I documented the conversation in the chart, so that the next time they came for an appointment, the doctor could acknowledge the passing of the child's grandmother.

A month later, Julia finally arrived for the checkup that she had missed three times. Who came along for the visit? Mom, Dad, and two grandmothers. I walked over to the dad and casually asked him who the women were. He pointed out each of them, saying, "That one is my mother, and the other one is my wife's mother. They came today because we are all going out for dinner together after Julia's appointment." Dad obviously had forgotten his excuse for missing last month's appointment. "Really?" I asked. "That's your mother-in-law? She looks wonderful!" Dad looked at me in a puzzled way and asked if I had met her before, as it was the first time she had come to our office. "No," I answered. "I've never met her. But last month, you told me the reason you forgot to call to cancel Julia's appointment was because your mother-in-law had died!" Poor Dad. He turned quite an interesting shade of red, while his eyes darted between me, his wife, and his mother-in-law, hoping that they had not heard any part of this conversation. And for those of you who are curious, no, I didn't bill him for the missed visit.

***

"My car was outside our apartment building, and right before I was about to leave to come to your office, someone threw a slab of marble counter over their balcony, attempting to drop it into the huge garbage receptacle below. They missed. It landed on my car."

And finally….

I always think it's cute when parents are shy or don't know what the real names of body parts are. Here are some examples:

Mom needed an appointment for her child because there seemed to be something stuck behind her "punching bag." When I asked where this punching bag was, mom said "at the back of her throat."

***

Mom called to say that her baby had a rash in his "baggage compartment."

***

Dad needed an appointment because his son had a severe rash on his "Mr. Wiggles."

***

A mother told the nurse that there seemed to be some soreness in the baby's "tool bag."

***